THE CUBAN MISSILE CRISIS THROUGH THE EYES OF JOHN F. KENNEDY

by Susan E. Hamen

Content Consultant
Renata Keller, PhD
Assistant Professor of International Relations
Boston University

Core Library

An Imprint of Abdo Publishing
abdopublishing.com

abdopublishing.com

Published by Abdo Publishing, a division of ABDO, PO Box 398166, Minneapolis, Minnesota 55439. Copyright © 2016 by Abdo Consulting Group, Inc. International copyrights reserved in all countries. No part of this book may be reproduced in any form without written permission from the publisher. Core Library™ is a trademark and logo of Abdo Publishing.

Printed in the United States of America, North Mankato, Minnesota
092015
012016

Cover Photo: AP Images
Interior Photos: AP Images, 1, 4, 9, 38; iStockphoto, 6; Cecil Stoughton/White House Photographs/John F. Kennedy Presidential Library and Museum, 11, 45; Harold Valentine/AP Images, 14; Bettmann/Corbis, 16, 18, 20, 29, 32, 37; Everett Collection/Newscom, 24; Red Line Editorial, 27; Sal Veder/AP Images, 34; Pablo Martinez Monsivais/AP Images, 40

Editor: Jon Westmark
Series Designer: Laura Polzin

Library of Congress Control Number: 2015945403

Cataloging-in-Publication Data
Hamen, Susan E.
 The Cuban Missile Crisis through the eyes of John F. Kennedy / Susan E. Hamen.
  p. cm. -- (Presidential perspectives)
ISBN 978-1-68078-031-4 (lib. bdg.)
Includes bibliographical references and index.
1. Cuban Missile Crisis, 1962--Juvenile literature.   2. Kennedy, John F. (John Fitzgerald), 1917-1963--Juvenile literature.   3. Presidents--United States--Juvenile literature.   I. Title.
973.922--dc23
                                                                            2015945403

CONTENTS

CHAPTER ONE

THE BRINK OF WAR

All day long, on October 22, 1962, newspapers, radios, and televisions alerted Americans that President John F. Kennedy would be giving an important speech that evening. People across the country sat in front of their televisions at 7:00 p.m. to hear the president's message. Many were nervous about what he would say. Kennedy gave his speech from the White House. He told Americans the Soviet

President John F. Kennedy addressed the nation on October 22, 1962.

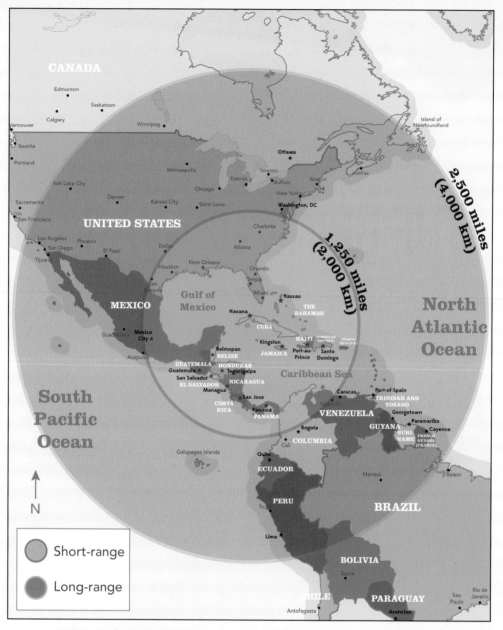

In Harm's Way

This map shows how close Cuba is to the United States.
Notice the range of the long-range and short-range missiles.
How far could the weapons reach? How do you think this
range affected Kennedy's decisions?

Union had built missile sites in Cuba, only 90 miles (145 km) south of Florida.

Kennedy's voice was calm but serious. He explained that the weapons Cuba was allowing the Soviet Union to bring there could fly great distances. Short-range missiles could travel far into the southern United States. Long-range weapons could reach as far north as Canada or as far south as Peru. These nuclear missiles could kill millions of people. But Kennedy assured his viewers, "One path we shall never choose, and that is the path of surrender or submission." Kennedy was determined to protect the United States. He announced that a quarantine, or blockade, would be set up. It would stop ships from going to Cuba. This would keep more Soviet military supplies from landing on the island.

"We have no wish to war with the Soviet Union," Kennedy said. But he added that any forceful act against the United States or its allies "will be met by whatever action is needed."

The Cold War

After World War II (1939–1945), the relationship between the United States and the Soviet Union was tense. The Allied forces had beaten Germany and its supporters in the war. The Allied countries consisted of the United States, the United Kingdom, France, the Soviet Union, and others. These nations split control of Germany after the war. Germany's capital city, Berlin, was also split in two.

An officer stands guard as workers build up the Berlin Wall in October 1961.

The Soviet Union was a communist country. Communism is a system in which the government controls the social and economic systems. Nikita Khrushchev took over as leader of the Soviet Union in 1953.

In August 1961, Khrushchev ordered a wall to be built that would divide Berlin. People caught trying to leave the communist part of Berlin were shot. The citizens of Berlin asked Kennedy for help. But there was nothing Kennedy could do. The Soviet Union would likely start a war with the United States if Kennedy stepped in.

The ongoing conflict between the United States and the Soviet Union became known as the Cold War. The two countries did not fight each other directly. But the threat of a war continued to grow. Many Americans feared that the Soviet Union would attack the United States. When they heard that the Soviets were bringing weapons to Cuba, many Americans believed a more serious war would break out.

Tensions Rise

The confrontation became known as the Cuban Missile Crisis. On the day of his speech, Kennedy sent a letter to Khrushchev. Kennedy explained that war would be bad for both countries.

The next morning, Kennedy arrived early at the White House. He had a meeting with a group of special advisers. The group was called the Executive Committee of the National Security Council

Kennedy leads a meeting of the ExComm during the Cuban Missile Crisis.

(ExComm). Khrushchev had not yet responded to Kennedy's speech about the blockade. Kennedy and his advisers felt that the Soviets could not be trusted.

Khrushchev responded by noon. He warned the United States against going ahead with the blockade. He said Kennedy's actions could lead to

John F. Kennedy

John Fitzgerald Kennedy was born on May 29, 1917, in Brookline, Massachusetts. His father, Joseph Kennedy Sr., was a wealthy banker. John served in the US Navy, the US House of Representatives, and the US Senate. He was elected president in 1961. He was the youngest US president in history. John was one of nine children. His brother Robert worked as the US attorney general. His brother Ted became an important US senator. John depended on his brother Robert's advice throughout the Cuban Missile Crisis.

terrible consequences. Kennedy knew that the United States needed a plan of action. There were 27 Soviet ships heading toward Cuba. Kennedy and the ExComm agreed to continue with their plan.

Later that night, Kennedy spoke with his brother Robert. He was the US attorney general and one of Kennedy's closest advisers. The brothers agreed the situation did not look good. Kennedy hoped the blockade was the right decision. If the ExComm made the wrong choice, millions of Americans could be in danger.

Kennedy won the presidential election in November 1960. On January 9, 1961, he gave his final speech in the Massachusetts state legislature. Here is a part of that speech:

> *Of those to whom much is given, much is required. And when at some future date the high court of history sits in judgment on each one of us . . . [it will ask] were we truly men of courage—with the courage to stand up to one's enemies—and the courage to stand up, when necessary, to one's associates . . . ? [W]ere we truly men of judgment . . . ? [W]ere we truly men of integrity—men who never ran out on either the principles in which they believed or the people who believed in them . . . ? Finally, were we truly men of dedication . . . ?*
>
> Source: John F. Kennedy. "City Upon a Hill Speech." Miller Center. University of Virginia, 2015. Web. Accessed May 8, 2015.

What's the Big Idea?

Kennedy spoke these words before taking office as president. It was many months before the Cuban Missile Crisis. What is the main point Kennedy is trying to make about being a leader? In what ways do you think the situation in Cuba defined how Kennedy would be judged?

A BUILDING THREAT

In the 1920s, Cuba became a popular vacation spot for Americans. Over time, Americans began investing in Cuban businesses. By the 1950s, Americans owned large portions of Cuban mines, public utilities, sugar plantations, and railroads. Cuba's economy depended heavily on the United States. Cuba's leader at the time was Fulgencio Batista. He welcomed US businesses in Cuba. The United States

Fulgencio Batista used military force to become leader of Cuba in 1952.

Castro, *right*, gives a speech during the Cuban Revolution in 1959.

supported Batista's rule because of this. But Batista did not always make choices based on what was best for his country. He often made decisions that would make money.

In 1953 a Cuban named Fidel Castro began a revolution. It overthrew Batista's government in 1959. As leader, Castro took control of many of the US businesses in Cuba. He did not pay Americans for them. The US started an embargo against Cuba. This meant the United States stopped trade between the two countries.

Castro limited freedom of speech in Cuba. Those who tried to fight for more freedom were often put in jail. Many Cubans left the country after Castro became leader. These people were called exiles.

The Bay of Pigs Invasion

In April 1960, the US Central Intelligence Agency (CIA) began training a group of exiles to be soldiers. The CIA developed a plan to bring the exiles back into Cuba to overthrow Castro. The plan was called the Bay of Pigs Invasion.

The invasion started on April 17, 1961. The plan failed. Nearly all the exiles were killed or captured. The attack caused Castro to further mistrust the United States. It also led Khrushchev to believe that Kennedy was inexperienced and weak. Kennedy admitted the plan had not been successful. But he also said the United States needed to continue to watch the situation in Cuba.

Captured soldiers march off to prison following the failed Bay of Pigs Invasion.

More Missiles

When Kennedy ran for president, many Americans believed that the Soviet Union had more nuclear missiles than the United States. Kennedy promised to raise defense spending if he became president. The spending would include building more missiles.

Khrushchev was determined to beat the United States in missile strength. He also wanted the United

States and its allies to leave Berlin. Khrushchev decided a solution would be to place missiles in Cuba. Khrushchev thought having missiles close to the United States would shift power in his country's favor. He hoped it would at least force Kennedy to consider pulling out of Berlin.

Operation Anadyr

Khrushchev spoke with Castro in 1962. He offered to place weapons in Cuba. The United States had carried out the Bay of Pigs attack just one year earlier. Castro feared that the United States would try to invade again. He agreed to Khrushchev's plan.

At first the plan was to set up weapons that could fire only 25 miles (40 km). But soon Khrushchev and Castro started planning to put long-range nuclear weapons in Cuba. The secret plan was known as Operation Anadyr. Few people knew what the two leaders were planning.

The first load of missiles arrived in Cuba on September 8, 1962. More were scheduled to follow.

Khrushchev, right, shakes hands with Cuban military leader Raúl Castro, Fidel's brother, in July 1962.

Rumors reached the United States of large weapons in Cuba. The Soviets insisted the weapons were only for defense.

The Truth Is Revealed

On October 14, 1962, a US spy plane flew over Cuba. The pilot photographed a Soviet missile site. He returned with 928 images. The photos confirmed that Cuba had nuclear missiles.

The CIA told Kennedy's national security adviser, McGeorge Bundy, the startling news. He showed Kennedy the photographs. Kennedy called a meeting with his advisers. They talked about actions the United States could take. They

Surveillance Missions

The US military limited surveillance of Cuba for five weeks in September 1962 for political reasons. The break slowed the discovery of the Soviet weapons. When spy-plane missions restarted, they found the weapon sites almost right away. Some people wondered if the crisis could have been avoided if the United States had seen the sites earlier.

PERSPECTIVES

Faking Sick

In the first days of the conflict, Kennedy tried to continue with his normal schedule. He did not want the public to learn that anything was wrong. He first wanted a better understanding of the situation. On October 20, Kennedy was in Chicago, Illinois. News reached him that the situation was getting worse. Kennedy was scheduled to appear in a number of US cities. But he decided to cancel his trip. He and his doctor came up with a story to avoid suspicion. They said Kennedy had a bad cold. The president pretended to be ill as he left his Chicago hotel and boarded a flight for Washington, DC.

agreed to meet later in the evening after a team at the US Department of Defense had time to think about the options for military action.

Until then, Kennedy had to continue his day. He attended a short church service to observe the National Day of Prayer. He then hosted a lunch for the crown prince of Libya. He pretended nothing was wrong. But he wondered as he went about his day what new information was coming to light.

Kennedy shared some of his thoughts in the meeting later that night. "We certainly have been wrong about what [Khrushchev is] trying to do in Cuba. . . . Not many of us thought that he was going to put [missiles] on Cuba." But the weapons were now on the island. New photos showed more sites. Kennedy knew the situation was more dangerous than they had thought.

EXPLORE ONLINE

Chapter Two talks about some of the events that led up to the Cuban Missile Crisis. The article below goes into more depth on this topic. It also includes a video that tells the story of the Cuban Missile Crisis. What new information did you learn after reading the article and watching the video?

Cuban Missile Crisis
mycorelibrary.com/john-f.-kennedy

TAKING A STAND

Kennedy and his advisers knew they had to come up with a plan quickly. With each passing hour, more missile sites were being built in Cuba. The group came up with some ideas. The options included threatening Castro, attacking Cuba, or doing nothing.

The heads of the US military branches, known as the Joint Chiefs of Staff, said the only option was to attack Cuba. But Defense Secretary Robert McNamara

Kennedy and McNamara meet outside the White House during the Cuban Missile Crisis.

presented a different option. He suggested they use the US Navy to isolate Cuba. US ships would surround the island. They would keep any ships carrying weapons from reaching Cuba. The men carefully weighed the options. Kennedy warned them, "If we stop one Russian ship, it means war. If we invade Cuba, it means war."

The Blockade Begins

On Sunday, October 21, the sixth day of the crisis, Kennedy received new information. It was from General Walter Sweeney of the Tactical Air Command. He reported that an air strike might not destroy all the missiles. Even if the United States attacked Cuba, Castro could possibly launch one of the missiles against the United States. Kennedy and his men decided the blockade was the best option.

The next morning, Kennedy officially established the ExComm, his special committee of advisers. Kennedy led the group. It would meet every morning at 10:00 a.m. throughout the crisis. Next Kennedy

Blocking the Way

The US Navy surrounded Cuba during the crisis. No ships coming from other countries could reach the country without being stopped. Which other island countries did the Navy surround? Why do you think it did that?

met with leaders of Congress. He told them of the situation in Cuba.

That evening Kennedy read his speech to the public. As he spoke, 180 US ships headed toward the Caribbean Sea. The blockade was beginning. Kennedy hoped Khrushchev would take his warnings seriously. Kennedy went to bed Monday night filled with concern and fear.

Khrushchev Responds

On Tuesday, October 23, Kennedy signed Proclamation 3504. The document authorized the blockade of Cuba. Kennedy prepared the rest of the US military for war. People readied bombers to strike both Cuba and the Soviet Union. Missile crews went on high alert. Kennedy awaited a Soviet response to his speech.

Khrushchev replied the following day. He said the Soviets considered the US blockade a violation of freedom of the seas. He warned Kennedy. If US ships stopped Soviet ships, it would be thought of as a hostile act. He

Stocking Up

Kennedy's televised speech shocked many Americans. Some rushed to buy groceries and other supplies. People wanted to be prepared in case the Soviets attacked the United States. Americans cleared grocery-store shelves of bottled water, canned goods, and radios. One store in Washington, DC, reported selling 900 cans of pemmican in two days. Pemmican is a raisin and nut food that is high in calories. Americans were unsure how the Cuban Missile Crisis would end. Many prepared for the worst.

Reporters take photos of Kennedy after he signs Proclamation 3504 on October 23, 1962.

added that his country was not afraid to protect its rights. Had Kennedy pushed the United States closer to war? The question hung over the president.

Turning Point

Fidel Castro was certain the United States would attack Cuba. He asked Khrushchev to strike the United States before it could invade Cuba. But Khrushchev was not ready to start war with the United States. Soon after Kennedy announced the blockade, Khrushchev ordered ships carrying missiles and other weapons to turn around.

Worldwide Worry

The leaders of other countries were nervous about how the Cuban Missile Crisis would end. A nuclear war would affect more than just the people of the United States, Cuba, and the Soviet Union. If missiles were launched at the Soviet Union, many European countries were also at risk. British philosopher Bertrand Russell sent Kennedy an angry telegram on October 23. In it he begged Kennedy to "end this madness." He condemned Kennedy's warning to the Soviets. Russell predicted it would end in war with many lives lost. "Your action [is a] . . . threat to human survival," he said in the message.

On October 26, the US Navy boarded a Lebanese ship close to Cuba. Officers searched the ship for weapons. The Soviet Union saw that the United States was serious about stopping ships. Later that day, Khrushchev sent a long letter to Kennedy. It was the eleventh day of the crisis. Khrushchev suggested a deal. The Soviet Union would remove the missiles in Cuba. In exchange the United States would stop blocking ships in the Caribbean. Khrushchev also asked the United States to promise it would not invade Cuba.

The next day, Kennedy received another message from the Soviets. In it Khrushchev demanded Kennedy remove US weapons from Turkey. The missiles in Turkey were capable of reaching the Soviet Union.

Kennedy felt that the situation was growing worse. The blockade had worked, but the missiles already in Cuba were still dangerous. Khrushchev's mixed messages made Kennedy wonder if the conflict could end peacefully.

FURTHER EVIDENCE

Chapter Three discusses Kennedy and the ExComm. It talks about how they had a hard time finding the right plan of action. Look through the pages at the website below. What evidence on the website supports the chapter's text?

John F. Kennedy and the Cuban Missile Crisis

mycorelibrary.com/john-f.-kennedy

CHAPTER FOUR

PROTECTING THE NATION

On October 27, more bad news arrived at the White House. Air Force pilot Major Rudolph Anderson Jr. had flown over Cuba to take photos of the missile sites. Surface-to-air missiles had shot down the plane and killed Anderson. Kennedy now knew the Soviets and Cubans were serious about using deadly force. They were bold enough to shoot down a US pilot taking photos. So Kennedy and

Cubans look over wreckage of an airplane on November 5, 1962. The wreck was thought to be a spy plane flown by Rudolph Anderson Jr.

A mother and her children practice going into a bomb shelter in their backyard. Many Americans created plans for what they would do during a nuclear attack.

his advisers feared they would not hesitate to use weapons against the United States. Kennedy told his men, "We are now in an entirely new ball game."

ExComm members insisted the United States must attack the missile sites the next morning. But Kennedy feared that such action would cause the Soviet Union to use missiles against the United States.

Kennedy and his advisers chose to send a telegram to Khrushchev. In it Kennedy mentioned Khrushchev's first letter. He ignored the second, more demanding letter. Kennedy said he hoped the two countries could come to a peaceful agreement. He promised to lift the blockade and not to invade Cuba if the weapons were taken apart.

The thought of millions of Americans being threatened by war, many of them children, weighed heavily on Kennedy's mind. He called the Air Force Reserve to active duty as he waited to hear back from Khrushchev. He wanted to

The "Hot Line"

Kennedy and Khrushchev communicated often throughout the 13 days of the crisis. But they had to wait for coded messages to be sent and received. After the Cuban Missile Crisis, a direct phone line was set up between the White House in Washington and the Kremlin, the center of Soviet government, in Moscow. It was called a "hot line." The line would ensure that the two countries could avoid declaring war due to slow communication.

PERSPECTIVES
Life as Usual

Many Americans were shocked and scared after hearing about the crisis. But it was a different story in Moscow. Khrushchev's son, Sergei, remembered, "For Americans it was a unique crisis, because it was the first time in all their history they realized they could be killed. For the Soviet people, they had their war experience. For them it was no different. There was no panic in the Moscow streets and life went on as usual."

avoid an invasion of Cuba at all costs. But he knew he must prepare for one.

Crisis Averted

On the morning of the thirteenth day of the conflict, the White House heard from Moscow, the Soviet capital. Khrushchev would be making a statement over the radio in Moscow. The US government was able to pick up the radio frequency. Analysts listened to Khrushchev's message and translated it. He had agreed to withdraw the missiles from Cuba in exchange for Kennedy's promise not to invade.

Thirteen days after Kennedy learned of dangerous weapons in Cuba, the conflict finally

A Soviet ship carries eight long-range missiles away from Cuba.

ended on October 28. Kennedy and the ExComm were deeply relieved. They had come dangerously close to war. They decided to leave the blockade in place until they could work out further details with the Soviets. Kennedy and Khrushchev were satisfied with the agreement. But Castro was upset. Khrushchev had agreed to remove the missiles from Cuba without

37

Kennedy, *right*, speaks with his brother Robert in October 1962. Robert was one of Kennedy's trusted advisers.

speaking with Castro first. Without the Soviet missiles, Cuba was once again vulnerable to US attack.

Kennedy wrote a telegram to Khrushchev confirming he had received the message. "Perhaps now, as we step back from danger, we can together make real progress," he wrote. That evening Kennedy chatted with his brother Robert. The president felt a great sense of relief for the first time in nearly two weeks. Many of his advisers had insisted the United States attack Cuba. But Kennedy knew he had made the right decision to work through the issue peacefully with Khrushchev. After the Soviet missiles had been taken down, Kennedy ordered that the US missiles in Turkey, and more in Italy, were to be taken apart.

After the Crisis

During the Cuban Missile Crisis, Kennedy proved to world leaders he would not back down if he were put in a position to defend his country. By November 20, 1962, Kennedy reported that the Soviets had taken down all missile sites in Cuba. Kennedy was pleased with the outcome. He said in a speech to the country that the achievement "might well open the door to the solution of other outstanding [world] problems."

The relationship between the United States and the Soviet Union was not perfect after the Cuban Missile Crisis. But both countries realized how close they had come to war. It helped them realize how important it was to discuss problems peacefully.

The relationship between the United States and Cuba did not improve for many years. Castro was very upset that the Soviet Union negotiated with

US President Barack Obama shakes hands with Cuban President Raúl Castro on April 11, 2015. Castro took over for his brother as leader of Cuba in February 2008.

the United States. But in December 2014, President Barack Obama said he would reestablish relations with Cuba. In August 2015, a member of the House of Representatives introduced a bill to stop the embargo against Cuba. After more than five decades, relations between the United States and Cuba seem to be improving.

After the Cuban Missile Crisis ended, Robert Kennedy wrote a book that told the story of what happened in the White House during those 13 days in October. He recalled:

> *On Tuesday morning, October 16, 1962 . . . President Kennedy called and asked me to come to the White House. He said only that we were facing great trouble. . . .*
>
> *That was the beginning of the Cuban missile crisis—a confrontation between the two giant atomic nations, the U.S. and the U.S.S.R., which brought the world to the abyss of nuclear destruction and the end of mankind. From that moment in President Kennedy's office until Sunday morning, October 28, that was my life—and for Americans and Russians, for the whole world, it was their life as well.*
>
> Source: Robert F. Kennedy. Thirteen Days: A Memoir of the Cuban Missile Crisis. New York: W. W. Norton Company, 1969. Print. 23.

Point of View

Robert Kennedy says the Cuban Missile Crisis became his life. Why do you think he says it was also the life of the whole world? Do you think he would have written this for the American public to read during the conflict? Why or why not?

IMPORTANT DATES

Jan. 1, 1959

Fidel Castro overthrows Cuba's leader, Fulgencio Batista, and becomes leader of Cuba.

April 1961

The United States sneaks Cuban exiles back into Cuba to overthrow Castro in a mission called the Bay of Pigs Invasion. The plan fails.

April 1962

Castro and Nikita Khrushchev begin to discuss installing long-range nuclear missiles in Cuba.

Oct. 22, 1962

Kennedy gives a televised speech to the American people informing them of the Cuban Missile Crisis and explaining that he had started a blockade of Cuba.

Oct. 24, 1962

Khrushchev orders Soviet ships carrying missiles and military gear to turn around.

Oct. 26, 1962

The US blockade stops a Lebanese ship. Khrushchev promises to remove the missiles if the United States promises not to invade Cuba.

Oct. 14, 1962

A US spy plane photographs Soviet missile sites in Cuba.

Oct. 21, 1962

President John F. Kennedy learns an airstrike of Cuba would not destroy all of the missiles. The remaining missiles would likely be used against the United States if it attacked.

Oct. 22, 1962

Kennedy officially establishes the ExComm, a committee of special advisers, to help him decide what to do about the crisis.

Oct. 27, 1962

Khrushchev demands that the United States remove missiles in Turkey. A US spy plane is shot down over Cuba. Kennedy's advisers push for a full attack.

Oct. 28, 1962

Khrushchev agrees to withdraw the missiles from Cuba. The 13-day Cuban Missile Crisis ends.

Nov. 20, 1962

The last of the Soviet missiles in Cuba are reported to have been taken apart.

STOP AND THINK

Tell the Tale

Chapter One of this book discusses Kennedy's speech to the American people about the Cuban Missile Crisis. It also explains the tense relationship between the United States and the Soviet Union. Imagine you are one of Kennedy's special advisers. Write 200 words about the conversations you had throughout the crisis with Kennedy, the other advisers, and Khrushchev. What do you suppose were some of Kennedy's biggest concerns?

Take a Stand

Some people believe that the United States becomes too involved in the political and governmental affairs of other countries. In recent history, the United States has sent troops to other countries and has become involved in distant wars. Do you think Kennedy and his staff had a good reason to blockade Cuba? Or do you think the United States overreacted?

Surprise Me

Chapter Three discusses Kennedy's reaction to the news of the Soviet missiles in Cuba. After reading this book, what two or three facts about Kennedy's decisions on how to handle the crisis did you find most surprising? Write a few sentences about each fact. Why did you find each fact surprising?

Dig Deeper

After reading this book, what questions do you still have about the Cuban Missile Crisis? With an adult's help, find a few reliable sources that can help you answer your questions. Write a paragraph about what you learned.

GLOSSARY

blockade
the closing off of an area to prevent anyone from entering or exiting

communism
a system in which the government owns all resources and distributes them among its citizens

crisis
a time of extreme difficulty or danger

embargo
to restrict something from being purchased or sold to another country

missile
a weapon that can be launched to strike a distant target

negotiate
to discuss with another party in order to arrange an agreement

nuclear
something that uses energy created by splitting atoms

surveillance
continual observation in order to gather information

telegram
a message sent by code through wires

LEARN MORE

Books

George, Enzo. *The Cold War*. Tarrytown, NY: Cavendish Square Publishing, 2016.

Gunderson, Megan M. *John F. Kennedy*. Edina, MN: Abdo Publishing, 2009.

Jeffrey, Gary. *The Cuban Missile Crisis*. New York: Crabtree Publishing, 2013.

Websites

To learn more about Presidential Perspectives, visit **booklinks.abdopublishing.com**. These links are routinely monitored and updated to provide the most current information available.

Visit **mycorelibrary.com** for additional free tools for teachers and students.

INDEX

ABOUT THE AUTHOR

Susan E. Hamen has written numerous children's books on various topics, including the Wright brothers, Pearl Harbor, World War II, the Industrial Revolution, and engineering. Hamen lives in Minnesota with her husband and two children.